My 61 US National Parks Bucket List Journal

Experience the 61 National Parks of the USA

Journal Delight

2019

Nr	State	Park	Date
1	Alaska	Denali	
2	Alaska	Gates of the Arctic	
3	Alaska	Glacier Bay	
4	Alaska	Katmai	
5	Alaska	Kenai Fjords	
6	Alaska	Kobuk Valley	
7	Alaska	Lake Clark	
8	Alaska	Wrangell - St. Elias	
9	American Samoa	American Samoa	
10	Arizona	Grand Canyon	
11	Arizona	Petrified Forest	
12	Arizona	Saguaro	
13	Arkansas	Hot Springs	
14	California	Channel Islands	
15	California	Death Valley	
16	California	Joshua Tree	
17	California	Kings Canyon	
18	California	Lassen Volcanic	
19	California	Pinnacles	
20	California	Redwood	
21	California	Sequoia	
22	California	Yosemite	
23	Colorado	Black Canyon of the Gunnison	
24	Colorado	Great Sand Dunes	
25	Colorado	Mesa Verde	
26	Colorado	Rocky Mountain	
27	Florida	Biscayne	
28	Florida	Dry Tortugas	
29	Florida	Everglades	
30	Hawaii	Haleakala	
31	Hawaii	Hawaii Volcanoes	

Nr	State	Park	Date
32	Indiana	Indiana Dunes	
33	Kentucky	Mammoth Cave	
34	Maine	Acadia	
35	Michigan	Isle Royale	
36	Minnesota	Voyageurs	
37	Missouri	Gateway Arch	
38	Montana	Glacier	
39	Nevada	Great Basin	
40	New Mexico	Carlsbad Caverns	
41	North Dakota	Theodore Roosevelt	
42	Ohio	Cuyahoga Valley	
43	Oregon	Crater Lake	
44	South Carolina	Congaree	
45	South Dakota	Badlands	
46	South Dakota	Wind Cave	
47	Tennessee, North Carolina	Great Smoky Mountains	
48	Texas	Big Bend	
49	Texas	Guadalupe Mountains	
50	Utah	Arches	
51	Utah	Bryce Canyon	
52	Utah	Canyonlands	
53	Utah	Capitol Reef	
54	Utah	Zion	
55	Virgin Islands	Virgin Islands	
56	Virginia	Shenandoah	
57	Washington	Mount Rainier	
58	Washington	North Cascades	
59	Washington	Olympic	
60	Wyoming	Grand Teton	
61	Wyoming, Idaho, Montana	Yellowstone	

Enjoy the beauty of the National Parks!

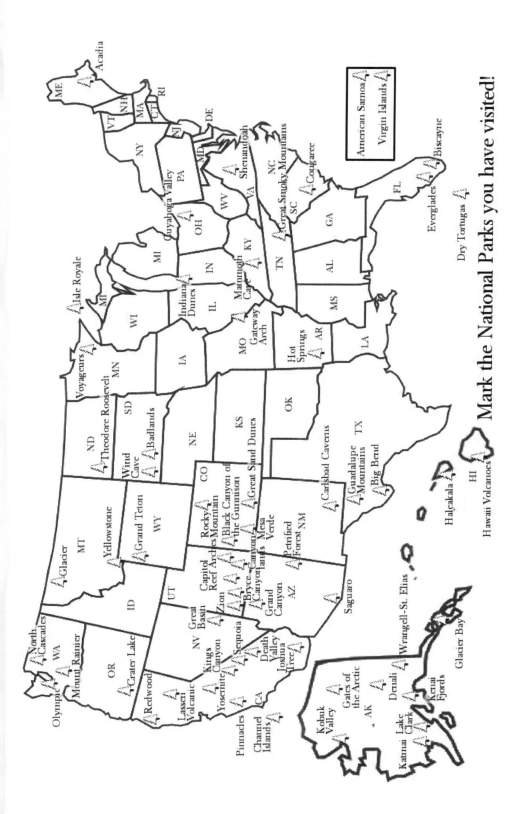

Mark the National Parks you have visited!

Top sightseeing spots:

_____

_____

_____

_____

_____

_____

What to explore:

_____

_____

_____

_____

_____

_____

Best place to camp:

Most scaring adventures:

_____

_____

_____

_____

_____

_____

DENALI

Est. 1917

Folks I know over there:

_____

_____

_____

Animals to look out for:

_____

_____

_____

I really want to experience:

_____

_____

_____

Souvenirs to take home:

_____

_____

_____

Best season to go there:

_____

I'm going to go there in:

_____

Temperature:

📅	Jan/Feb	Mar/Apr	May/Jun	Jul/Aug	Sep/Oct	Nov/Dec
🌡						

DENALI

Notes

Time I spent over there:

Most enjoyed:

Most hillarious experience:

Missed this time but really need to go there next time:

Friends I have made:

Contact details:

Top sightseeing spots:

What to explore:

Best place to camp:

Most scaring adventures:

GATES OF THE ARCTIC

Est. 1980

Folks I know over there:

_____

_____

_____

Animals to look out for:

_____

_____

_____

I really want to experience:

_____

_____

_____

Souvenirs to take home:

_____

_____

_____

Best season to go there:

_____

I'm going to go there in:

_____

Temperature:

1	Jan/Feb	Mar/Apr	May/Jun	Jul/Aug	Sep/Oct	Nov/Dec
🌡						

GATES OF THE ARCTIC

Time I spent over there:

Most enjoyed:

_____

Most hillarious experience:

_____

_____

Missed this time but really need to go there next time:

_____

_____

_____

Friends I have made:

Contact details:

_____

_____

_____

Top sightseeing spots:

What to explore:

Best place to camp:

Most scaring adventures:

GLACIER BAY

Est. 1980

Folks I know over there:

Animals to look out for:

I really want to experience:

Souvenirs to take home:

Best season to go there:

I'm going to go there in:

Temperature:

1	Jan/Feb	Mar/Apr	May/Jun	Jul/Aug	Sep/Oct	Nov/Dec
🌡						

GLACIER BAY

Notes

Time I spent over there:

Most enjoyed:

Most hillarious experience:

Missed this time but really need to go there next time:

Friends I have made:

Contact details:

Top sightseeing spots:

What to explore:

Best place to camp:

Most scaring adventures:

KATMAI

Est. 1980

Folks I know over there:

_____

_____

_____

Animals to look out for:

_____

_____

_____

I really want to experience:

_____

_____

_____

Souvenirs to take home:

_____

_____

_____

Best season to go there:

_____

I'm going to go there in:

_____

Temperature:

🔢	Jan/Feb	Mar/Apr	May/Jun	Jul/Aug	Sep/Oct	Nov/Dec
🌡						

KATMAI

Time I spent over there:

Most enjoyed:

Most hillarious experience:

Missed this time but really need to go there next time:

Friends I have made:

Contact details:

Top sightseeing spots:

--- ---

--- ---

--- ---

What to explore:

--- ---

--- ---

--- ---

Best place to camp: Most scaring adventures:

--- ---

--- ---

--- ---

KENAI FJORDS

Est. 1980

Folks I know over there:

Animals to look out for:

I really want to experience:

Souvenirs to take home:

Best season to go there:

I'm going to go there in:

Temperature:

1	Jan/Feb	Mar/Apr	May/Jun	Jul/Aug	Sep/Oct	Nov/Dec
🌡						

KENAI FJORDS

Notes

Time I spent over there:

_____

Most enjoyed:

_____

Most hillarious experience:

_____

_____

Missed this time but really need to go there next time:

_____

_____

_____

_____

_____

Friends I have made:

_____

_____

Contact details:

_____

_____

Top sightseeing spots:

What to explore:

Best place to camp:

Most scaring adventures:

KOBUK VALLEY

Est. 1980

Folks I know over there:

_____

_____

_____

Animals to look out for:

_____

_____

_____

I really want to experience:

_____

_____

Souvenirs to take home:

_____

_____

Best season to go there:

_____

I'm going to go there in:

_____

Temperature:

🌡	Jan/Feb	Mar/Apr	May/Jun	Jul/Aug	Sep/Oct	Nov/Dec

KOBUK VALLEY

Notes

Time I spent over there:

Most enjoyed:

Most hillarious experience:

Missed this time but really need to go there next time:

Friends I have made:

Contact details:

Top sightseeing spots:

What to explore:

Best place to camp:

Most scaring adventures:

LAKE CLARK

Est. 1980

Folks I know over there:

....

....

....

Animals to look out for:

....

....

....

I really want to experience:

....

....

....

Souvenirs to take home:

....

....

....

Best season to go there:

....

I'm going to go there in:

....

Temperature:

1	Jan/Feb	Mar/Apr	May/Jun	Jul/Aug	Sep/Oct	Nov/Dec
🌡						

LAKE CLARK

Notes

Time I spent over there:

Most enjoyed:

Most hillarious experience:

Missed this time but really need to go there next time:

Friends I have made:

Contact details:

Planning
08

Top sightseeing spots:

What to explore:

Best place to camp:

Most scaring adventures:

WRANGELL - ST. ELIAS

Est. 1980

Folks I know over there:

_____

_____

_____

Animals to look out for:

_____

_____

_____

I really want to experience:

_____

_____

_____

Souvenirs to take home:

_____

_____

_____

Best season to go there:

_____

I'm going to go there in:

_____

Temperature:

🌡	Jan/Feb	Mar/Apr	May/Jun	Jul/Aug	Sep/Oct	Nov/Dec

WRANGELL - ST. ELIAS

Time I spent over there:

Most enjoyed:

Most hillarious experience:

Missed this time but really need to go there next time:

Friends I have made:

Contact details:

Top sightseeing spots:

....

....

....

What to explore:

....

....

....

Best place to camp: Most scaring adventures:

....

....

....

AMERICAN SAMOA

Est. 1988

Folks I know over there:

_____

_____

_____

Animals to look out for:

_____

_____

_____

I really want to experience:

_____

_____

_____

Souvenirs to take home:

_____

_____

_____

Best season to go there:

_____

I'm going to go there in:

_____

Temperature:

🗓1	Jan/Feb	Mar/Apr	May/Jun	Jul/Aug	Sep/Oct	Nov/Dec
🌡						

AMERICAN SAMOA

Notes

Time I spent over there:

....

Most enjoyed:

....

Most hillarious experience:

....

....

Missed this time but really need to go there next time:

....

....

....

....

....

....

Friends I have made:

....

....

....

Contact details:

....

....

....

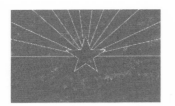

Top sightseeing spots:

_____   _____

_____   _____

_____   _____

What to explore:

_____   _____

_____   _____

_____   _____

Best place to camp: Most scaring adventures:

_____   _____

_____   _____

_____   _____

GRAND CANYON

Est. 1919

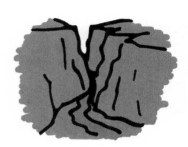

Folks I know over there:

_____

_____

_____

Animals to look out for:

_____

_____

_____

I really want to experience:

_____

_____

_____

Souvenirs to take home:

_____

_____

_____

Best season to go there:

_____

I'm going to go there in:

_____

Temperature:

1	Jan/Feb	Mar/Apr	May/Jun	Jul/Aug	Sep/Oct	Nov/Dec
🌡						

GRAND CANYON

Time I spent over there:

Most enjoyed:

Most hillarious experience:

Missed this time but really need to go there next time:

Friends I have made:

Contact details:

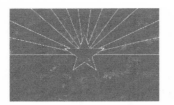

Top sightseeing spots:

What to explore:

Best place to camp:

Most scaring adventures:

PETRIFIED FOREST

Est. 1962

Folks I know over there:

....

....

....

Animals to look out for:

....

....

....

I really want to experience:

....

....

....

Souvenirs to take home:

....

....

....

Best season to go there:

....

I'm going to go there in:

....

Temperature:

🌡	Jan/Feb	Mar/Apr	May/Jun	Jul/Aug	Sep/Oct	Nov/Dec
🌡						

PETRIFIED FOREST

Notes

Time I spent over there:

....

Most enjoyed:

....

Most hillarious experience:

....

....

Missed this time but really need to go there next time:

....

....

....

....

Friends I have made:

....

....

....

Contact details:

....

....

....

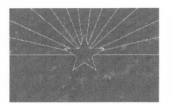

Top sightseeing spots:

What to explore:

Best place to camp:

Most scaring adventures:

SAGUARO

Est. 1994

Folks I know over there:

_____

_____

_____

Animals to look out for:

_____

_____

_____

I really want to experience:

_____

_____

_____

Souvenirs to take home:

_____

_____

_____

Best season to go there:

_____

I'm going to go there in:

_____

Temperature:

1	Jan/Feb	Mar/Apr	May/Jun	Jul/Aug	Sep/Oct	Nov/Dec
🌡						

SAGUARO

Time I spent over there:

Most enjoyed:

Most hillarious experience:

Missed this time but really need to go there next time:

Friends I have made:

Contact details:

Planning

13

Top sightseeing spots:

What to explore:

Best place to camp:

Most scaring adventures:

HOT SPRINGS

Est. 1921

Folks I know over there:

....

....

....

Animals to look out for:

....

....

....

I really want to experience:

....

....

....

Souvenirs to take home:

....

....

....

Best season to go there:

....

I'm going to go there in:

....

Temperature:

1	Jan/Feb	Mar/Apr	May/Jun	Jul/Aug	Sep/Oct	Nov/Dec
🌡						

HOT SPRINGS

Notes

Time I spent over there:

Most enjoyed:

....

....

Most hillarious experience:

....

....

Missed this time but really need to go there next time:

....

....

....

....

....

....

Friends I have made:

Contact details:

....

....

....

....

....

....

CALIFORNIA REPUBLIC

Top sightseeing spots:

What to explore:

Best place to camp:

Most scaring adventures:

CHANNEL ISLANDS

Est. 1980

Folks I know over there:

Animals to look out for:

I really want to experience:

Souvenirs to take home:

Best season to go there:

I'm going to go there in:

Temperature:

🗓	Jan/Feb	Mar/Apr	May/Jun	Jul/Aug	Sep/Oct	Nov/Dec
🌡						

CHANNEL ISLANDS *Notes*

Time I spent over there:

Most enjoyed:

_____

_____

Most hillarious experience:

_____

_____

Missed this time but really need to go there next time:

_____

_____

_____

_____

_____

_____

Friends I have made:

Contact details:

_____

_____

_____

_____

_____

_____

CALIFORNIA REPUBLIC

Top sightseeing spots:

What to explore:

Best place to camp:

Most scaring adventures:

DEATH VALLEY

Est. 1994

Folks I know over there:

....

....

....

Animals to look out for:

....

....

I really want to experience:

....

....

Souvenirs to take home:

....

....

Best season to go there:

....

I'm going to go there in:

....

Temperature:

📅	Jan/Feb	Mar/Apr	May/Jun	Jul/Aug	Sep/Oct	Nov/Dec
🌡						

DEATH VALLEY

Time I spent over there:

Most enjoyed:

Most hillarious experience:

Missed this time but really need to go there next time:

Friends I have made:

Contact details:

CALIFORNIA REPUBLIC

Top sightseeing spots:

What to explore:

Best place to camp:

Most scaring adventures:

JOSHUA TREE

Est. 1994

Folks I know over there:

....

....

....

Animals to look out for:

....

....

....

I really want to experience:

....

....

....

Souvenirs to take home:

....

....

....

Best season to go there:

....

I'm going to go there in:

....

Temperature:

1	Jan/Feb	Mar/Apr	May/Jun	Jul/Aug	Sep/Oct	Nov/Dec

JOSHUA TREE

Notes

Time I spent over there:

Most enjoyed:

Most hillarious experience:

Missed this time but really need to go there next time:

Friends I have made:

Contact details:

CALIFORNIA REPUBLIC

Planning

17

Top sightseeing spots:

What to explore:

Best place to camp:

Most scaring adventures:

KINGS CANYON

Est. 1940

Folks I know over there:

_____

_____

_____

Animals to look out for:

_____

_____

_____

I really want to experience:

_____

_____

Souvenirs to take home:

_____

_____

Best season to go there:

_____

I'm going to go there in:

_____

Temperature:

1	Jan/Feb	Mar/Apr	May/Jun	Jul/Aug	Sep/Oct	Nov/Dec
🌡						

KINGS CANYON

Notes

Time I spent over there:

Most enjoyed:

Most hillarious experience:

Missed this time but really need to go there next time:

Friends I have made:

Contact details:

CALIFORNIA REPUBLIC

Top sightseeing spots:

What to explore:

Best place to camp:

Most scaring adventures:

LASSEN VOLCANIC

Est. 1916

Folks I know over there:

_____

_____

_____

Animals to look out for:

_____

_____

_____

I really want to experience:

_____

_____

_____

Souvenirs to take home:

_____

_____

_____

Best season to go there:

_____

I'm going to go there in:

_____

Temperature:

1	Jan/Feb	Mar/Apr	May/Jun	Jul/Aug	Sep/Oct	Nov/Dec
🌡						

LASSEN VOLCANIC

Notes

Time I spent over there:

_____

Most enjoyed:

_____

Most hillarious experience:

_____

_____

Missed this time but really need to go there next time:

_____

_____

_____

_____

_____

_____

Friends I have made:

_____

_____

_____

Contact details:

_____

_____

_____

CALIFORNIA REPUBLIC

Top sightseeing spots:

What to explore:

Best place to camp:

Most scaring adventures:

PINNACLES

Est. 2013

Folks I know over there:

_____

_____

_____

Animals to look out for:

_____

_____

_____

I really want to experience:

_____

_____

_____

Souvenirs to take home:

_____

_____

_____

Best season to go there:

_____

I'm going to go there in:

_____

Temperature:

🗓	Jan/Feb	Mar/Apr	May/Jun	Jul/Aug	Sep/Oct	Nov/Dec
🌡						

PINNACLES

Time I spent over there:

Most enjoyed:

Most hillarious experience:

Missed this time but really need to go there next time:

Friends I have made:

Contact details:

CALIFORNIA REPUBLIC

Top sightseeing spots:

What to explore:

Best place to camp:

Most scaring adventures:

REDWOOD

Est. 1968

Folks I know over there:

_____

_____

_____

Animals to look out for:

_____

_____

_____

I really want to experience:

_____

_____

_____

Souvenirs to take home:

_____

_____

_____

Best season to go there:

_____

I'm going to go there in:

_____

Temperature:

1	Jan/Feb	Mar/Apr	May/Jun	Jul/Aug	Sep/Oct	Nov/Dec
🌡						

REDWOOD

Time I spent over there:

Most enjoyed:

Most hillarious experience:

Missed this time but really need to go there next time:

Friends I have made:

Contact details:

CALIFORNIA REPUBLIC

Top sightseeing spots:

What to explore:

Best place to camp:

Most scaring adventures:

SEQUOIA

Est. 1890

Folks I know over there:

....

....

....

Animals to look out for:

....

....

....

I really want to experience:

....

....

....

Souvenirs to take home:

....

....

....

Best season to go there:

....

I'm going to go there in:

....

Temperature:

1	Jan/Feb	Mar/Apr	May/Jun	Jul/Aug	Sep/Oct	Nov/Dec
🌡						

SEQUOIA

Time I spent over there:

Most enjoyed:

Most hillarious experience:

Missed this time but really need to go there next time:

Friends I have made:

Contact details:

CALIFORNIA REPUBLIC

Top sightseeing spots:

What to explore:

Best place to camp:

Most scaring adventures:

YOSEMITE

Est. 1890

Folks I know over there:

_____

_____

_____

Animals to look out for:

_____

_____

_____

I really want to experience:

_____

_____

_____

Souvenirs to take home:

_____

_____

_____

Best season to go there:

_____

I'm going to go there in:

_____

Temperature:

i	Jan/Feb	Mar/Apr	May/Jun	Jul/Aug	Sep/Oct	Nov/Dec
🌡						

YOSEMITE

Time I spent over there:

Most enjoyed:

Most hillarious experience:

Missed this time but really need to go there next time:

Friends I have made:

Contact details:

Top sightseeing spots:

_____

_____

_____

_____

_____

_____

What to explore:

_____

_____

_____

_____

_____

_____

Best place to camp: Most scaring adventures:

_____

_____

_____

_____

_____

_____

BLACK CANYON OF THE GUNNISON

Est. 1999

Folks I know over there:

_____

_____

_____

Animals to look out for:

_____

_____

_____

I really want to experience:

_____

_____

_____

Souvenirs to take home:

_____

_____

_____

Best season to go there:

_____

I'm going to go there in:

_____

Temperature:

1	Jan/Feb	Mar/Apr	May/Jun	Jul/Aug	Sep/Oct	Nov/Dec
🌡						

BLACK CANYON OF THE GUNNISON

Notes

Time I spent over there:

....

Most enjoyed:

....

Most hillarious experience:

....

....

Missed this time but really need to go there next time:

....

....

....

....

....

....

Friends I have made:

....

....

....

Contact details:

....

....

....

Top sightseeing spots:

_____   _____

_____   _____

_____   _____

What to explore:

_____   _____

_____   _____

_____   _____

Best place to camp: Most scaring adventures:

_____   _____

_____   _____

_____   _____

GREAT SAND DUNES

Est. 2004

Folks I know over there:

_____

_____

_____

Animals to look out for:

_____

_____

_____

I really want to experience:

_____

_____

_____

Souvenirs to take home:

_____

_____

_____

Best season to go there:

_____

I'm going to go there in:

_____

Temperature:

1	Jan/Feb	Mar/Apr	May/Jun	Jul/Aug	Sep/Oct	Nov/Dec
🌡						

GREAT SAND DUNES *Notes*

Time I spent over there:

Most enjoyed:

Most hillarious experience:

Missed this time but really need to go there next time:

Friends I have made:

Contact details:

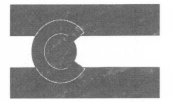

Top sightseeing spots:

What to explore:

Best place to camp:

Most scaring adventures:

MESA VERDE

Est. 1906

Folks I know over there:

_____

_____

_____

Animals to look out for:

_____

_____

_____

I really want to experience:

_____

_____

_____

Souvenirs to take home:

_____

_____

_____

Best season to go there:

_____

I'm going to go there in:

_____

Temperature:

1	Jan/Feb	Mar/Apr	May/Jun	Jul/Aug	Sep/Oct	Nov/Dec
🌡						

MESA VERDE

Time I spent over there:

Most enjoyed:

_____

Most hillarious experience:

_____

_____

Missed this time but really need to go there next time:

_____

_____

_____

Friends I have made:

Contact details:

_____

_____

_____

Top sightseeing spots:

What to explore:

Best place to camp:

Most scaring adventures:

ROCKY MOUNTAIN

Est. 1915

Folks I know over there:

_____

_____

_____

Animals to look out for:

_____

_____

_____

I really want to experience:

_____

_____

_____

Souvenirs to take home:

_____

_____

_____

Best season to go there:

_____

I'm going to go there in:

_____

Temperature:

1	Jan/Feb	Mar/Apr	May/Jun	Jul/Aug	Sep/Oct	Nov/Dec
🌡						

ROCKY MOUNTAIN

Notes

Time I spent over there:

_____

Most enjoyed:

_____

Most hillarious experience:

_____

_____

Missed this time but really need to go there next time:

_____

_____

_____

_____

_____

_____

Friends I have made:

_____

_____

_____

Contact details:

_____

_____

_____

Top sightseeing spots:

What to explore:

Best place to camp:

Most scaring adventures:

BISCAYNE

Est. 1980

Folks I know over there:

_____

_____

_____

Animals to look out for:

_____

_____

_____

I really want to experience:

_____

_____

_____

Souvenirs to take home:

_____

_____

_____

Best season to go there:

_____

I'm going to go there in:

_____

Temperature:

📅	Jan/Feb	Mar/Apr	May/Jun	Jul/Aug	Sep/Oct	Nov/Dec
🌡						

BISCAYNE

Notes

Time I spent over there:

Most enjoyed:

_____

_____

Most hillarious experience:

_____

_____

Missed this time but really need to go there next time:

_____

_____

_____

_____

_____

_____

Friends I have made:

Contact details:

_____

_____

_____

_____

_____

_____

Top sightseeing spots:

What to explore:

Best place to camp:

Most scaring adventures:

DRY TORTUGAS

Est. 1992

Folks I know over there:

_____

_____

_____

Animals to look out for:

_____

_____

_____

I really want to experience:

_____

_____

_____

Souvenirs to take home:

_____

_____

_____

Best season to go there:

_____

I'm going to go there in:

_____

Temperature:

📅	Jan/Feb	Mar/Apr	May/Jun	Jul/Aug	Sep/Oct	Nov/Dec
🌡						

DRY TORTUGAS

Notes

Time I spent over there:

Most enjoyed:

Most hillarious experience:

Missed this time but really need to go there next time:

Friends I have made:

Contact details:

Top sightseeing spots:

What to explore:

Best place to camp:

Most scaring adventures:

EVERGLADES

Est. 1947

Folks I know over there:

....

....

....

Animals to look out for:

....

....

....

I really want to experience:

....

....

....

Souvenirs to take home:

....

....

....

Best season to go there:

....

I'm going to go there in:

....

Temperature:

1	Jan/Feb	Mar/Apr	May/Jun	Jul/Aug	Sep/Oct	Nov/Dec
🌡						

EVERGLADES

Time I spent over there:

Most enjoyed:

Most hillarious experience:

Missed this time but really need to go there next time:

Friends I have made:

Contact details:

Top sightseeing spots:

What to explore:

Best place to camp:

Most scaring adventures:

HALEAKALA

Est. 1916

Folks I know over there:

_____

_____

_____

Animals to look out for:

_____

_____

_____

I really want to experience:

_____

_____

_____

Souvenirs to take home:

_____

_____

_____

Best season to go there:

_____

I'm going to go there in:

_____

Temperature:

1	Jan/Feb	Mar/Apr	May/Jun	Jul/Aug	Sep/Oct	Nov/Dec
🌡						

HALEAKALA

Time I spent over there:

Most enjoyed:

Most hillarious experience:

Missed this time but really need to go there next time:

Friends I have made:

Contact details:

Top sightseeing spots:

What to explore:

Best place to camp:

Most scaring adventures:

HAWAII VOLCANOES

Est. 1916

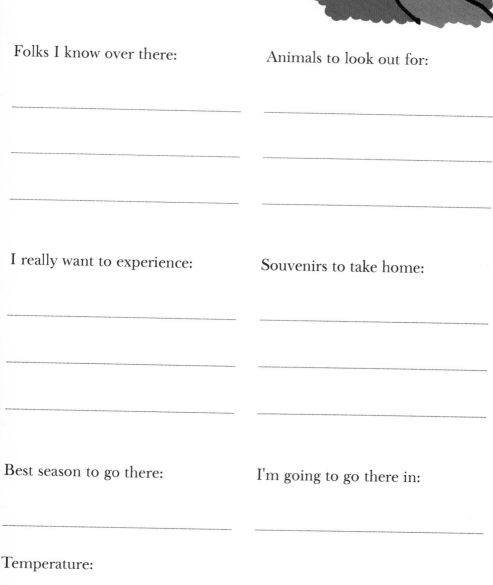

Folks I know over there:

_____

_____

_____

Animals to look out for:

_____

_____

_____

I really want to experience:

_____

_____

_____

Souvenirs to take home:

_____

_____

_____

Best season to go there:

_____

I'm going to go there in:

_____

Temperature:

	Jan/Feb	Mar/Apr	May/Jun	Jul/Aug	Sep/Oct	Nov/Dec

HAWAII VOLCANOES

Notes

Time I spent over there:

Most enjoyed:

Most hillarious experience:

Missed this time but really need to go there next time:

Friends I have made:

Contact details:

Top sightseeing spots:

_____   _____

_____   _____

_____   _____

What to explore:

_____   _____

_____   _____

_____   _____

Best place to camp: Most scaring adventures:

_____   _____

_____   _____

_____   _____

INDIANA DUNES

Est. 2019

Folks I know over there:

_____

_____

_____

Animals to look out for:

_____

_____

_____

I really want to experience:

_____

_____

_____

Souvenirs to take home:

_____

_____

_____

Best season to go there:

_____

I'm going to go there in:

_____

Temperature:

1	Jan/Feb	Mar/Apr	May/Jun	Jul/Aug	Sep/Oct	Nov/Dec

INDIANA DUNES

Time I spent over there:

Most enjoyed:

Most hillarious experience:

Missed this time but really need to go there next time:

Friends I have made:

Contact details:

Top sightseeing spots:

_____   _____

_____   _____

_____   _____

What to explore:

_____   _____

_____   _____

_____   _____

Best place to camp: Most scaring adventures:

_____   _____

_____   _____

_____   _____

MAMMOTH CAVE

Est. 1941

Folks I know over there:

....

....

....

Animals to look out for:

....

....

....

I really want to experience:

....

....

....

Souvenirs to take home:

....

....

....

Best season to go there:

....

I'm going to go there in:

....

Temperature:

1	Jan/Feb	Mar/Apr	May/Jun	Jul/Aug	Sep/Oct	Nov/Dec
🌡						

MAMMOTH CAVE

Notes

Time I spent over there:

_____

Most enjoyed:

_____

Most hillarious experience:

_____

_____

Missed this time but really need to go there next time:

_____

_____

_____

_____

_____

_____

Friends I have made:

_____

_____

Contact details:

_____

_____

Top sightseeing spots:

What to explore:

Best place to camp:

Most scaring adventures:

ACADIA

Est. 1919

Folks I know over there:

_____

_____

_____

Animals to look out for:

_____

_____

_____

I really want to experience:

_____

_____

_____

Souvenirs to take home:

_____

_____

_____

Best season to go there:

_____

I'm going to go there in:

_____

Temperature:

1	Jan/Feb	Mar/Apr	May/Jun	Jul/Aug	Sep/Oct	Nov/Dec
🌡						

ACADIA

Time I spent over there:

Most enjoyed:

Most hillarious experience:

Missed this time but really need to go there next time:

Friends I have made:

Contact details:

Top sightseeing spots:

_____   _____

_____   _____

_____   _____

What to explore:

_____   _____

_____   _____

_____   _____

Best place to camp: Most scaring adventures:

_____   _____

_____   _____

_____   _____

ISLE ROYALE

Est. 1940

Folks I know over there:

_____

_____

_____

Animals to look out for:

_____

_____

_____

I really want to experience:

_____

_____

_____

Souvenirs to take home:

_____

_____

_____

Best season to go there:

_____

I'm going to go there in:

_____

Temperature:

1	Jan/Feb	Mar/Apr	May/Jun	Jul/Aug	Sep/Oct	Nov/Dec
🌡						

ISLE ROYALE

Notes

Time I spent over there:

Most enjoyed:

Most hillarious experience:

Missed this time but really need to go there next time:

Friends I have made:

Contact details:

Top sightseeing spots:

_____   _____

_____   _____

_____   _____

What to explore:

_____   _____

_____   _____

_____   _____

Best place to camp: Most scaring adventures:

_____   _____

_____   _____

_____   _____

VOYAGEURS

Est. 1975

Folks I know over there:

_____

_____

_____

Animals to look out for:

_____

_____

_____

I really want to experience:

_____

_____

_____

Souvenirs to take home:

_____

_____

_____

Best season to go there:

_____

I'm going to go there in:

_____

Temperature:

🌡	Jan/Feb	Mar/Apr	May/Jun	Jul/Aug	Sep/Oct	Nov/Dec

VOYAGEURS

Time I spent over there:

_____

Most enjoyed:

_____

Most hillarious experience:

_____

_____

Missed this time but really need to go there next time:

_____

_____

_____

_____

Friends I have made:

_____

_____

_____

Contact details:

_____

_____

_____

Top sightseeing spots:

_____   _____

_____   _____

_____   _____

What to explore:

_____   _____

_____   _____

_____   _____

Best place to camp: Most scaring adventures:

_____   _____

_____   _____

_____   _____

GATEWAY ARCH

Est. 2018

Folks I know over there:

_____

_____

_____

Animals to look out for:

_____

_____

_____

I really want to experience:

_____

_____

_____

Souvenirs to take home:

_____

_____

_____

Best season to go there:

_____

I'm going to go there in:

_____

Temperature:

1	Jan/Feb	Mar/Apr	May/Jun	Jul/Aug	Sep/Oct	Nov/Dec

GATEWAY ARCH

Notes

Time I spent over there:

Most enjoyed:

Most hillarious experience:

Missed this time but really need to go there next time:

Friends I have made:

Contact details:

Top sightseeing spots:

_____   _____

_____   _____

_____   _____

What to explore:

_____   _____

_____   _____

_____   _____

Best place to camp: Most scaring adventures:

_____   _____

_____   _____

_____   _____

GLACIER

Est. 1910

Folks I know over there:

_____

_____

_____

Animals to look out for:

_____

_____

_____

I really want to experience:

_____

_____

_____

Souvenirs to take home:

_____

_____

_____

Best season to go there:

_____

I'm going to go there in:

_____

Temperature:

🌡	Jan/Feb	Mar/Apr	May/Jun	Jul/Aug	Sep/Oct	Nov/Dec
🌡						

GLACIER

Time I spent over there:

Most enjoyed:

Most hillarious experience:

Missed this time but really need to go there next time:

Friends I have made:

Contact details:

Top sightseeing spots:

What to explore:

Best place to camp:

Most scaring adventures:

GREAT BASIN

Est. 1986

Folks I know over there:

_____

_____

_____

Animals to look out for:

_____

_____

_____

I really want to experience:

_____

_____

_____

Souvenirs to take home:

_____

_____

_____

Best season to go there:

_____

I'm going to go there in:

_____

Temperature:

1	Jan/Feb	Mar/Apr	May/Jun	Jul/Aug	Sep/Oct	Nov/Dec
🌡						

GREAT BASIN

Time I spent over there:

Most enjoyed:

Most hillarious experience:

Missed this time but really need to go there next time:

Friends I have made:

Contact details:

Top sightseeing spots:

What to explore:

Best place to camp:

Most scaring adventures:

CARLSBAD CAVERNS

Est. 1930

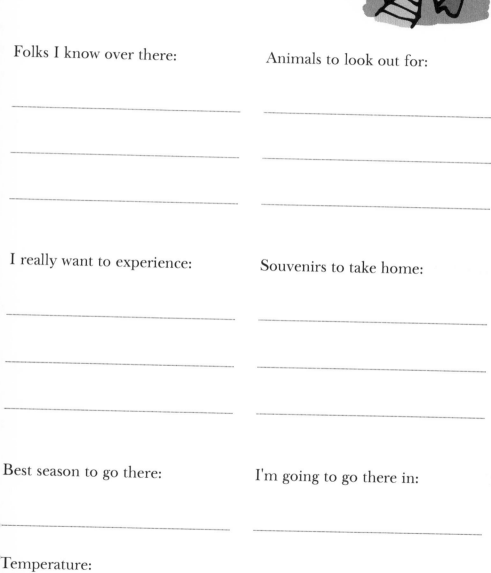

Folks I know over there:

_____

_____

_____

Animals to look out for:

_____

_____

_____

I really want to experience:

_____

_____

_____

Souvenirs to take home:

_____

_____

_____

Best season to go there:

_____

I'm going to go there in:

_____

Temperature:

🌡	Jan/Feb	Mar/Apr	May/Jun	Jul/Aug	Sep/Oct	Nov/Dec

CARLSBAD CAVERNS   *Notes*

Time I spent over there:

_____

Most enjoyed:

_____

Most hillarious experience:

_____

_____

Missed this time but really need to go there next time:

_____   _____

_____   _____

_____   _____

Friends I have made:

_____

_____

_____

Contact details:

_____

_____

_____

Top sightseeing spots:

_____   _____

_____   _____

_____   _____

What to explore:

_____   _____

_____   _____

_____   _____

Best place to camp: Most scaring adventures:

_____   _____

_____   _____

_____   _____

THEODORE ROOSEVELT

Est. 1978

Folks I know over there:

....

....

....

Animals to look out for:

....

....

....

I really want to experience:

....

....

....

Souvenirs to take home:

....

....

....

Best season to go there:

....

I'm going to go there in:

....

Temperature:

1	Jan/Feb	Mar/Apr	May/Jun	Jul/Aug	Sep/Oct	Nov/Dec
🌡						

THEODORE ROOSEVELT

Time I spent over there:

Most enjoyed:

Most hillarious experience:

Missed this time but really need to go there next time:

Friends I have made:

Contact details:

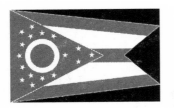

Top sightseeing spots:

What to explore:

Best place to camp:

Most scaring adventures:

CUYAHOGA VALLEY

Est. 2000

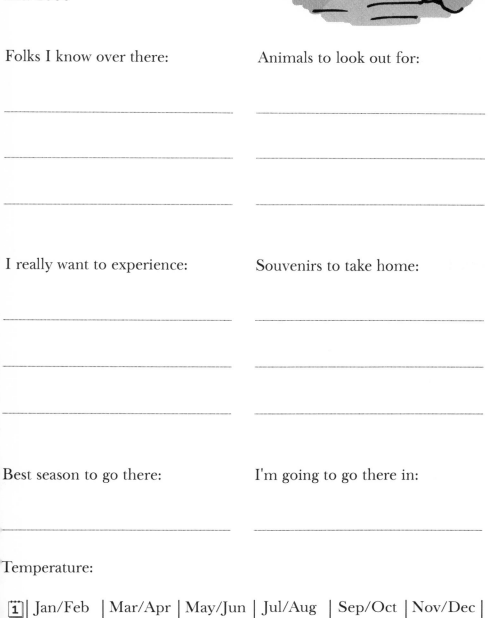

Folks I know over there:

Animals to look out for:

I really want to experience:

Souvenirs to take home:

Best season to go there:

I'm going to go there in:

Temperature:

1	Jan/Feb	Mar/Apr	May/Jun	Jul/Aug	Sep/Oct	Nov/Dec
🌡						

CUYAHOGA VALLEY *Notes*

Time I spent over there:

Most enjoyed:

Most hillarious experience:

Missed this time but really need to go there next time:

Friends I have made:

Contact details:

Top sightseeing spots:

What to explore:

Best place to camp:

Most scaring adventures:

CRATER LAKE

Est. 1902

Folks I know over there:

_____

_____

_____

Animals to look out for:

_____

_____

_____

I really want to experience:

_____

_____

_____

Souvenirs to take home:

_____

_____

_____

Best season to go there:

_____

I'm going to go there in:

_____

Temperature:

1	Jan/Feb	Mar/Apr	May/Jun	Jul/Aug	Sep/Oct	Nov/Dec
🌡						

CRATER LAKE

Notes

Time I spent over there:

Most enjoyed:

Most hillarious experience:

Missed this time but really need to go there next time:

Friends I have made:

Contact details:

Top sightseeing spots:

What to explore:

Best place to camp:

Most scaring adventures:

CONGAREE

Est. 2003

Folks I know over there:

....

....

....

Animals to look out for:

....

....

....

I really want to experience:

....

....

....

Souvenirs to take home:

....

....

....

Best season to go there:

....

I'm going to go there in:

....

Temperature:

1	Jan/Feb	Mar/Apr	May/Jun	Jul/Aug	Sep/Oct	Nov/Dec
🌡						

CONGAREE

Time I spent over there:

Most enjoyed:

Most hillarious experience:

Missed this time but really need to go there next time:

Friends I have made:

Contact details:

Top sightseeing spots:

_____

_____

_____

What to explore:

_____

_____

_____

Best place to camp:

_____

_____

Most scaring adventures:

_____

_____

BADLANDS

Est. 1978

Folks I know over there:

....

....

....

Animals to look out for:

....

....

....

I really want to experience:

....

....

....

Souvenirs to take home:

....

....

....

Best season to go there:

....

I'm going to go there in:

....

Temperature:

1	Jan/Feb	Mar/Apr	May/Jun	Jul/Aug	Sep/Oct	Nov/Dec
🌡						

BADLANDS

Time I spent over there:

Most enjoyed:

Most hillarious experience:

Missed this time but really need to go there next time:

Friends I have made:

Contact details:

46

Top sightseeing spots:

What to explore:

Best place to camp:

Most scaring adventures:

WIND CAVE

Est. 1903

Folks I know over there:

_____

_____

_____

Animals to look out for:

_____

_____

_____

I really want to experience:

_____

_____

_____

Souvenirs to take home:

_____

_____

_____

Best season to go there:

_____

I'm going to go there in:

_____

Temperature:

1	Jan/Feb	Mar/Apr	May/Jun	Jul/Aug	Sep/Oct	Nov/Dec
🌡						

WIND CAVE

Time I spent over there:

Most enjoyed:

....

....

Most hillarious experience:

....

....

Missed this time but really need to go there next time:

....

....

....

....

....

....

Friends I have made:

Contact details:

....

....

....

....

....

....

Top sightseeing spots:

What to explore:

Best place to camp:

Most scaring adventures:

GREAT SMOKY MOUNTAINS

Est. 1934

Folks I know over there:

....

....

....

Animals to look out for:

....

....

....

I really want to experience:

....

....

....

Souvenirs to take home:

....

....

....

Best season to go there:

....

I'm going to go there in:

....

Temperature:

1	Jan/Feb	Mar/Apr	May/Jun	Jul/Aug	Sep/Oct	Nov/Dec

GREAT SMOKY MOUNTAINS

Time I spent over there:

Most enjoyed:

_____

_____

Most hillarious experience:

_____

_____

Missed this time but really need to go there next time:

_____

_____

_____

_____

Friends I have made:

Contact details:

_____

_____

_____

_____

Top sightseeing spots:

....

....

....

What to explore:

....

....

....

Best place to camp: Most scaring adventures:

....

....

BIG BEND

Est. 1944

Folks I know over there:

....

....

....

Animals to look out for:

....

....

....

I really want to experience:

....

....

....

Souvenirs to take home:

....

....

....

Best season to go there:

....

I'm going to go there in:

....

Temperature:

1	Jan/Feb	Mar/Apr	May/Jun	Jul/Aug	Sep/Oct	Nov/Dec

BIG BEND

Time I spent over there:

Most enjoyed:

....

....

Most hillarious experience:

....

....

Missed this time but really need to go there next time:

....

....

....

....

....

....

Friends I have made:

Contact details:

....

....

....

....

....

....

Top sightseeing spots:

What to explore:

Best place to camp:

Most scaring adventures:

GUADALUPE MOUNTAINS

Est. 1966

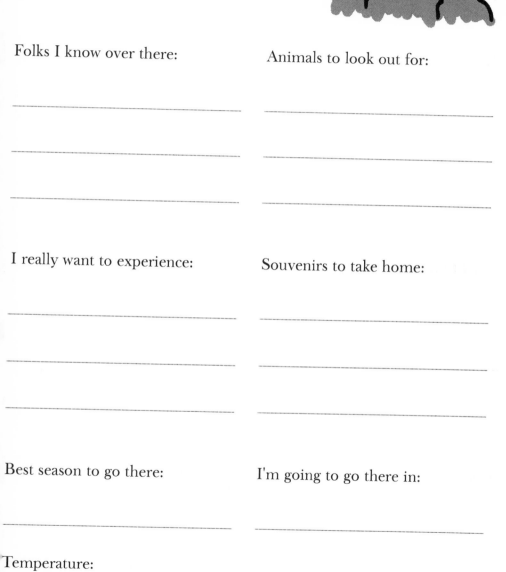

Folks I know over there:

....

....

....

Animals to look out for:

....

....

....

I really want to experience:

....

....

....

Souvenirs to take home:

....

....

....

Best season to go there:

....

I'm going to go there in:

....

Temperature:

1	Jan/Feb	Mar/Apr	May/Jun	Jul/Aug	Sep/Oct	Nov/Dec
🌡						

GUADALUPE MOUNTAINS

Notes

Time I spent over there:

_____

Most hillarious experience:

_____

_____

Missed this time but really need to go there next time:

_____

_____

_____

Most enjoyed:

_____

_____

_____

Friends I have made:

_____

_____

_____

Contact details:

_____

_____

_____

Top sightseeing spots:

_____   _____

_____   _____

_____   _____

What to explore:

_____   _____

_____   _____

_____   _____

Best place to camp: Most scaring adventures:

_____   _____

_____   _____

_____   _____

ARCHES

Est. 1971

Folks I know over there:

Animals to look out for:

I really want to experience:

Souvenirs to take home:

Best season to go there:

I'm going to go there in:

Temperature:

🌡	Jan/Feb	Mar/Apr	May/Jun	Jul/Aug	Sep/Oct	Nov/Dec

ARCHES

Time I spent over there:

Most enjoyed:

_____

Most hillarious experience:

_____

_____

Missed this time but really need to go there next time:

_____   _____

_____   _____

_____   _____

Friends I have made:

Contact details:

_____   _____

_____   _____

Top sightseeing spots:

What to explore:

Best place to camp:

Most scaring adventures:

BRYCE CANYON

Est. 1928

Folks I know over there:

....

....

....

Animals to look out for:

....

....

....

I really want to experience:

....

....

....

Souvenirs to take home:

....

....

....

Best season to go there:

....

I'm going to go there in:

....

Temperature:

1	Jan/Feb	Mar/Apr	May/Jun	Jul/Aug	Sep/Oct	Nov/Dec

BRYCE CANYON

Notes

Time I spent over there:

Most enjoyed:

Most hillarious experience:

Missed this time but really need to go there next time:

Friends I have made:

Contact details:

Top sightseeing spots:

What to explore:

Best place to camp:

Most scaring adventures:

CANYONLANDS

Est. 1964

Folks I know over there:

....

....

....

Animals to look out for:

....

....

....

I really want to experience:

....

....

....

Souvenirs to take home:

....

....

....

Best season to go there:

....

I'm going to go there in:

....

Temperature:

1	Jan/Feb	Mar/Apr	May/Jun	Jul/Aug	Sep/Oct	Nov/Dec
🌡						

CANYONLANDS

Notes

Time I spent over there:

Most enjoyed:

....

....

Most hillarious experience:

....

....

Missed this time but really need to go there next time:

....

....

....

....

....

....

Friends I have made:

Contact details:

....

....

....

....

Top sightseeing spots:

_____   _____

_____   _____

_____   _____

What to explore:

_____   _____

_____   _____

_____   _____

Best place to camp: Most scaring adventures:

_____   _____

_____   _____

_____   _____

CAPITOL REEF

Est. 1971

Folks I know over there:

....

....

....

Animals to look out for:

....

....

....

I really want to experience:

....

....

....

Souvenirs to take home:

....

....

....

Best season to go there:

....

I'm going to go there in:

....

Temperature:

1	Jan/Feb	Mar/Apr	May/Jun	Jul/Aug	Sep/Oct	Nov/Dec
🌡						

CAPITOL REEF

Time I spent over there:

Most enjoyed:

_____

Most hillarious experience:

_____

_____

Missed this time but really need to go there next time:

_____

_____

_____

Friends I have made:

Contact details:

_____

_____

Top sightseeing spots:

What to explore:

Best place to camp:

Most scaring adventures:

ZION

Est. 1919

Folks I know over there:

....

....

....

Animals to look out for:

....

....

....

I really want to experience:

....

....

....

Souvenirs to take home:

....

....

....

Best season to go there:

....

I'm going to go there in:

....

Temperature:

1	Jan/Feb	Mar/Apr	May/Jun	Jul/Aug	Sep/Oct	Nov/Dec
🌡						

ZION

Time I spent over there:

Most enjoyed:

_____

_____

Most hillarious experience:

_____

_____

Missed this time but really need to go there next time:

_____

_____

_____

_____

Friends I have made:

Contact details:

_____

_____

_____

_____

Top sightseeing spots:

What to explore:

Best place to camp:

Most scaring adventures:

VIRGIN ISLANDS

Est. 1956

Folks I know over there:

Animals to look out for:

I really want to experience:

Souvenirs to take home:

Best season to go there:

I'm going to go there in:

Temperature:

1	Jan/Feb	Mar/Apr	May/Jun	Jul/Aug	Sep/Oct	Nov/Dec

VIRGIN ISLANDS

Notes

Time I spent over there:

Most enjoyed:

Most hillarious experience:

Missed this time but really need to go there next time:

Friends I have made:

Contact details:

Top sightseeing spots:

What to explore:

Best place to camp:

Most scaring adventures:

SHENANDOAH

Est. 1935

Folks I know over there:

....

....

....

Animals to look out for:

....

....

....

I really want to experience:

....

....

....

Souvenirs to take home:

....

....

....

Best season to go there:

....

I'm going to go there in:

....

Temperature:

1	Jan/Feb	Mar/Apr	May/Jun	Jul/Aug	Sep/Oct	Nov/Dec

SHENANDOAH

Notes

Time I spent over there:

Most enjoyed:

Most hillarious experience:

Missed this time but really need to go there next time:

Friends I have made:

Contact details:

Top sightseeing spots:

_____

_____

_____

_____

_____

_____

What to explore:

_____

_____

_____

_____

_____

_____

Best place to camp: Most scaring adventures:

_____

_____

_____

_____

_____

_____

MOUNT RAINIER

Est. 1899

Folks I know over there:

_____

_____

_____

Animals to look out for:

_____

_____

_____

I really want to experience:

_____

_____

_____

Souvenirs to take home:

_____

_____

_____

Best season to go there:

_____

I'm going to go there in:

_____

Temperature:

🗓	Jan/Feb	Mar/Apr	May/Jun	Jul/Aug	Sep/Oct	Nov/Dec
🌡						

MOUNT RAINIER

Notes

Time I spent over there:

Most enjoyed:

Most hillarious experience:

Missed this time but really need to go there next time:

Friends I have made:

Contact details:

Top sightseeing spots:

What to explore:

Best place to camp:

Most scaring adventures:

NORTH CASCADES

Est. 1968

Folks I know over there:

....

....

....

Animals to look out for:

....

....

....

I really want to experience:

....

....

....

Souvenirs to take home:

....

....

....

Best season to go there:

....

I'm going to go there in:

....

Temperature:

1	Jan/Feb	Mar/Apr	May/Jun	Jul/Aug	Sep/Oct	Nov/Dec

NORTH CASCADES

Notes

Time I spent over there:

_____

Most enjoyed:

_____

Most hillarious experience:

_____

_____

Missed this time but really need to go there next time:

_____

_____

_____

_____

_____

_____

Friends I have made:

_____

_____

Contact details:

_____

_____

Top sightseeing spots:

What to explore:

Best place to camp:

Most scaring adventures:

OLYMPIC

Est. 1938

Folks I know over there:

Animals to look out for:

I really want to experience:

Souvenirs to take home:

Best season to go there:

I'm going to go there in:

Temperature:

🌡	Jan/Feb	Mar/Apr	May/Jun	Jul/Aug	Sep/Oct	Nov/Dec
🌡						

OLYMPIC

Time I spent over there:

Most enjoyed:

Most hillarious experience:

Missed this time but really need to go there next time:

Friends I have made:

Contact details:

Top sightseeing spots:

What to explore:

Best place to camp:

Most scaring adventures:

GRAND TETON

Est. 1929

Folks I know over there:

_____

_____

_____

Animals to look out for:

_____

_____

_____

I really want to experience:

_____

_____

Souvenirs to take home:

_____

_____

Best season to go there:

_____

I'm going to go there in:

_____

Temperature:

📅	Jan/Feb	Mar/Apr	May/Jun	Jul/Aug	Sep/Oct	Nov/Dec
🌡						

GRAND TETON

Notes

Time I spent over there:

_____

Most enjoyed:

_____

Most hillarious experience:

_____

_____

Missed this time but really need to go there next time:

_____

_____

_____

_____

_____

_____

Friends I have made:

_____

_____

_____

Contact details:

_____

_____

_____

Top sightseeing spots:

What to explore:

Best place to camp:

Most scaring adventures:

YELLOWSTONE

Est. 1872

Folks I know over there:

_____

_____

_____

Animals to look out for:

_____

_____

_____

I really want to experience:

_____

_____

_____

Souvenirs to take home:

_____

_____

_____

Best season to go there:

_____

I'm going to go there in:

_____

Temperature:

🌡	Jan/Feb	Mar/Apr	May/Jun	Jul/Aug	Sep/Oct	Nov/Dec
🌡						

YELLOWSTONE

Notes

Time I spent over there:

Most enjoyed:

Most hillarious experience:

Missed this time but really need to go there next time:

Friends I have made:

Contact details:

Made in the USA
Middletown, DE
16 October 2020